The Little Red Book of Teacher Attributes

Loretta G. Weisberg

by Loretta G. Weisberg

So You Want to Be a Teacher
The Little Red Book of Teacher Attributes
Loretta G. Weisberg

info@writingise-z.com | www.writingise-z.com

Library of Congress Control Number
TXu 1-943-287

Cover & Page Design by HeadsUp Marketing.
Illustrations by Mari Braswell.

Copyright © 2015 Loretta G. Weisberg.
All rights reserved. No portion of this book may be
reproduced without written permission of the author.

ISBN: 978-0-9887194-1-5

First Edition

Dedication

I would like to dedicate this little red book of teacher attributes to the children and teachers who work together in concert towards the journey ahead of them.

NOTHING HAPPENS
　　　　　　　　WITHOUT A TEACHER

To Lynn,
　　Your expertise make this happen — I'm so grateful.
—Thank you!
　　Love & Hugs,
　　　Loretta

Table of Contents

I: Do No Harm

1. Control and Power 2
2. Mind Games 4
3. Words Matter 6
4. Tales of Tribulation 8
5. The Problem Solver 10
6. The Changer 12
7. Making Judgments 14
8. The Self-Righteous 16
9. Do You See Me? 18

II: Forget About It

10. Get Over It 22
11. Grudges 24
12. The Elephant Memory 26
13. Don't Take It Personally 28
14. The Achilles' Heel 30
15. Now, It's Personal 32
16. Yes, But 34
17. Leave It at the Door 36
18. How Are You, Today? 38

So You Want to Be a Teacher

III: There Are Strategies in Here, Somewhere

19. Find the Start Button 42
20. Keep Going Back 44
21. Move It 46
22. It's You and Me, Kid 48
23. Stop It---Or, Else!!! 50
24. Catch 'Em Being Good 54
25. Is This Important? 56
26. Correct Those Papers 58
27. The Challenger (Make Them Think) 60
28. Inspire Them 62
29. Expectations 64
30. What's a Memory Worth? 66
31. Say What!? 70

IV: You're On---Break-A-Leg

32. Your World Is a Stage 74
33. Just a Wild and Crazy Guy 76
34. All Grown Up—YIKES!!! 78
35. Justice-Oriented 80
36. Teacher and Student 82
37. What Is This Thing Called Research? 84

38.	Who Are You Hanging With? 86
39.	The Advocate 88
40.	Sympathy Versus Empathy 90
41.	Definitely—Maybe—Never Again! 94
42.	Rejuvenate 96
43.	What's This Called? 98
44.	A Million or Bust 100
45.	Who's on First? 102
46.	Hindsight 104
47.	Hope and Faith 106
48.	And One More -- Mercy 108
49.	Do No Harm. 110

So You Want to Be a Teacher

1: Do No Harm

Control and Power

Use control and power carefully.

Interact in ways that demonstrate fairness with the students.

Refrain from forcing your will and creating confrontations with students. When you feel a tightening and the sensation of increasing heat in the pit of your stomach, you're attempting to force your will. Evaluate your interactions with students to insure they are not some deep-seated, misguided extensions of, "Me, grown-up; you, kid" or "I'm the grown-up, now—it's my turn" or "I run the show!"

Remember, by virtue of age and experience, you are the adult. Power and control are in your hands and so is how you choose to use them.

They may forget what you said
but they will never forget
how you made them feel.

~ Anonymous
The Gigantic Book of Teacher Wisdom

Mind Games

- Bullying with words, gestures, facial expressions or actions

- Jokes at the expense of a student

- Making fun of a student

- Using sarcasm

- Demonstrating frustration, annoyance, irritation, or exasperation

Students have neither the command of the language nor the life experiences to defend themselves. This puts students at a distinct disadvantage in their attempts to shield themselves from damaging adult interactions. Such harmful actions by adults could contribute to a student being bullied, negatively labeled or nicknamed by others. Also, since self-concept is evolving, students do not have the self-assurance to define themselves. They may well believe the authority figure, in this case, the teacher's characterization, whether true or not. Bear in mind what a student exhibits today may be obscure tomorrow. People evolve, but the characterizations made by others may hinder, even impede, the process.

Do not provoke your children, Lest they become discouraged.

Colossians 3:21

Words Matter

If we wouldn't say it to an adult, why would we say it to a child?

Tales of Tribulation

Gossiping about students or their parents is unfair because,

... it's prejudicial.

... it's biased.

... it doesn't allow for the student/parent to defend himself or herself.

... it colors the opinions of others.

... its opinions are slow to change.

... it assassinates a person's character.

... it doesn't offer solutions.

"If you can't say something nice, don't say anything at all," still works.

The Problem Solver

Students come to us with all kinds of issues, puzzle pieces if you will. Some pieces are easily figured out, others are not. We usually cannot solve the problems students face outside of the school environment. Our job, then, is to provide the most positive and interesting environment, within our power. Offer the alternative. Be the nurturer. Create a school climate that is irresistible, one that is constructive, optimistic, enthusiastic, and has value. What's that saying? Oh, yes, "Build it and they will come."

Most of us are willing to change, not because we see the light, but because we feel the heat.

~ Anonymous

The Changer

Accept the child where he or she is -- academically, socially, and emotionally; and how he or she is -- the good, the bad, and the ugly.

Refrain from the desire, hope, or determination to change the child. Let change be that of the child's journey. Model, example, and instruct in behavioral generalities, but refrain from concluding that part of your mission is to change a student in some way. Attempting to yank a student from his or her value system, attitudes, behaviors, or perspectives to life responses deemed more appropriate, doesn't work. Change is a process and cannot be demanded. Students need time to evolve and the freedom to grow at their own pace. Seek to clarify your underlying motives and perspectives in attempts to bring about changes in a student because, in doing so, comes the realization that the only person you can change is you.

Everything that irritates us
about others can lead us to
an understanding of ourselves.

~ Carl Gustov Jung

Making Judgments

Whether we are passing judgment on students, parents, or co-workers, be careful; we might be looking in the mirror.

No one can save us but ourselves.
No one can and no one may.
We ourselves must walk the path.

~ Buddha

The Self-Righteous

You might be adamantly convinced of the rightness of your actions and beliefs but so are others convinced of theirs.

Refrain from the impulse to proselytize. Instilling the religious foundation and/or belief system for a child is a parental right. Parents can extend a religious denomination of choice, or not. They decide on the belief system to instill. Teachers are not given the same status or legal right in determining the religious directives or personal philosophies for students. Teachers demonstrate what it means to be a good citizen in the mini-society of school. They characterize appropriate manners, social graces, universal values, and decorum but need to leave the teaching of individual convictions and/or religious doctrines to the institutions of family and religion.

A great many people
think they are thinking
when they are merely
rearranging their prejudices.

~ William James

Do You See Me?

Void of evidence, no matter how you jumble up preconceived ideas, anticipation, speculation, and personal opinions; they still drop into slots of misconceptions, even prejudice. Observe, listen, and suspend judgment. Strive to be open, give students the benefit of the doubt, recognize and celebrate their emerging self-hood. Be intent in discovering where each student is coming from and how they perceive themselves. Help students to discover their individual talents and uniqueness. After all, growing up is universal, exemplifies change, and, at times, a difficult process. We've all been there.

II: Forget About It

Get Over It

The lesson didn't work the way it was supposed to: three students argued over computer time, the principal needed the information before noon, lunch was interrupted by a parent; and now, you accidently dropped that whole jumbo box of thumb tacks that you just had to have all over the floor. Stop cussing! Throw your head back and laugh! It's just one of those days and tomorrow is only hours away!

The heaviest thing you can carry
... is a grudge.

~ Author Unknown

Grudges

Dismiss, let go, even forgive, not for them but for you. Each new day, start anew.

The Elephant Memory

A well-instituted behavior management plan is your blueprint for acceptable classroom behavior and productive student experiences. But like all of us, the intellect knows the "shoulds," but the emotions can entice the "shouldn'ts," and, even with the best behavior management plan, students will misbehave. Speak to the behavioral issue at hand - the whys and the why nots. No matter how tempting, refrain from reminding students of their every transgression since setting eyes on them. You've heard about an elephant's memory and the proverbial kitchen sink syndrome, right? Enough said.

Don't Take It Personally

There are many reasons why a student misbehaves. He or she may be seeking attention. Other issues could include wrestling with a problem, difficulty with an assignment, dealings with peers, serious problems at home, or feeling lonely, depressed, and/or anxious; the list goes on and on. Very likely, the one area that's not a problem is having you for a teacher. The student has a safe and non-threatening environment to act out and you're just there to catch his or her rays of discontent. If it weren't you, it would be someone else, equally safe. If the child were an adult, the response could easily be, "It's not you---it's me." Refrain from confronting, demanding, or creating conflict. Instead, diffuse the situation and seek to redirect. Work to establish a positive relationship, identify the student's issue(s) and offer solutions. Two brief perspectives:

➤ No child is born angry or misbehaving.

➤ Given the choice to be happy and successful or miserable and a failure, the choice is clear.

Don't take student misbehavior as a personal insult or attack, in other words, don't take it personally.

Forget About It

The Achilles' Heel

There comes a time when a student will crash into your emotional Achilles' heel. It may be the student's attempt to exercise power and control or, perhaps, issues of oppositional or defiant behavior. You may not even recognize your Achilles' heel until you experience the situation that results in your losing self-control. But, it is important to identify what can really set you off. It might be feeling that your efforts, status, or values are under attack or you are personally under assault, without justification. Maybe it's feeling that you are the butt of ridicule and/or rudeness. Whatever it is, identifying your emotional Achilles' heel weakens its influence in a confrontational situation. Understanding what can really get to you diminishes the need to protect your inner-self when under assault and, instead of a major, reactionary, emotional response on your part, a cooler, rational approach prevails. You are able to deal with the student in a practical manner and speak to the issue(s) rather than react based upon your emotional Achilles' heel.

To accept good advice is but to increase one's ability.

~ Johann Wolfgang von Goethe

Now, It's Personal

➢ Your colleagues offer suggestions, techniques, methods, materials, strategies, and/or advice.

➢ Parents imply.

➢ Students indicate.

Consider each, evaluate each, and, if found useful, utilize them. Someone taking the time to offer constructive criticism or advice wishes you success. That's a gift and now, it's personal.

The end of a matter is better
than the beginning,
and patience is better than pride.

Ecclesiastes 7:8

Yes, But

If you find yourself formulating your response, anxious to state your comments, convinced that you are right, or certain that your ideas are more pertinent, you are half-listening, half-understanding, and hardly considering another point of view. You are, instead, impeding the sincerity of communication. You are mentally articulating the "yes-buts" of your convictions. This is especially a lost opportunity when conversing with students but applies to co-workers and parents, as well, because it's observing the meanings and body language behind the words that offer the most insight. At times, out of the need to be right or the conviction of our correctness, we mentally dismiss the comments of others, especially when conversing with students. Sometimes, however, we don't need to prove that we're right; we just need to be quiet.

Leave It at the Door

If we have not a problem in the world, guess where we might find ourselves. Everyone has trials and tribulations; sometimes, situations test everything about us. But you need to become an expert in suspending problems while in the school environment for your success and the success of your students. You cannot manage or resolve the problem while at school. The problem will be there at the end of the school day, taking a break from trying to solve the problem may be of greater benefit in considering solutions, and, as their teacher, students deserve your undivided attention. Instead of dwelling, get totally involved and swept up into the day's activities. Forget yourself and focus on the students and the work at hand. That's what students need. That's what they deserve. That's what they're entitled to expect. There are unintended consequences, of a teacher weighted down with a personal problem - for you, for the students, and for the learning environment. Negativity compromises. Learn to compartmentalize. Stick your problems in a mental box, close it for now, and leave it at the door.

How Are You, Today?

Students need to count on the constancy of your characteristics. They need to be able to have confidence in your approachability. They need to trust that your emotional responses are consistent and reliable. The vicissitudes of teacher interaction is frustrating, fear-inducing, and confusing. Students have no choice but to be in school—it's required. We, as teachers, are in loco parentis, "in place of the parent." We need to ask ourselves if we would want our child, younger sibling, favorite niece/nephew, or cousin to spend time in our room. Figuratively speaking, testing the waters or throwing a hat in the ring as the barometer for determining the mood of the teacher, is unfair. It casts a shadow of doubt and anxiety over the students and makes for an uncomfortable classroom environment. Smile, take an interest, notice little things to compliment, be positive and above all, be even-keeled. Your students will know what mood you're in without needing to determine or mentally ask, "How are you, today?"

Forget About It

III: There Are Strategies in Here, Somewhere

It's always better to ask
than to make an assumption.

~ Don Miguel Ruiz

Find the Start Button

Find out what students know before asking them to learn something new. Assume nothing. Instead, verify; too easy-move up a space, too hard-move back a space, just right -- pass Go!

Better to take small steps
in the right direction
than to make a great leap
only to stumble backward.

Old Chinese Proverb

Keep Going Back

Facial expressions are fantastic! That quizzical or pained look tells volumes about confusion. When facing perplexing, cork-screw expressions, your students are having a lesson melt-down; so, break it down and teach the lesson in smaller increments. Break it down, down, and down until you see that "Light in their eyes;" that "Aha" moment and those three wonderful, little words, "I get it!" I knew a teacher who boasted that she could break down shoe-lace tying into 100 incremental lessons. I often wondered about that, but I got the point.

Move It

A desk is very handy for storing, filing, organizing. It's least valuable for sitting.

Stand up and teach—keep moving!

It's You and Me, Kid

A student will hardly remember the lesson in years to come; but, personal attention is a keeper. It may be surprising to know that some students have little opportunity to interact with the adults in his or her life; however, that opportunity can be readily available at school--with you, the teacher. One-on-one is a miracle worker. It builds understanding, camaraderie, and a relationship between student and teacher. A bit of advice: be an active listener. Use eye-contact, gestures, and utterances, give your full attention, pertinent feedback, and comments. Just imagine, you have the power to make a child feel validated and special; now, how neat is that!

Anyone can steer the ship
. . . when the sea is calm.

~ Publilius Syrus

Stop It---Or, Else!!!

Demanding behavior doesn't work. Commanding students to stop disruptive behavior followed by the teacher's consequence statements opens the door to a power struggle. Redirect, remind, diffuse, use the numerous Best Practices in developing a classroom management plan and stick to it. Develop an arsenal of behavioral strategies. The least effective approach is the attempt to stop the behavior with minimal interaction and as quickly as possible in order to resume class. Instead, turn the situation into a teaching moment. Instruct rather than force or threaten. Children do not have an automatic knowledge of appropriate behavior. Rather, appropriate behavior is taught. It is discussed and demonstrated. As teachers, we have the responsibility of providing students with opportunities and strategies to develop appropriate behavior and help move them toward independent selection of acceptable behavior in a variety of social situations.

Children need limits and boundaries. Learning the rules of conduct for themselves and others and how to function within their environment and the larger society helps them feel safe and accepted. Limits and boundaries contribute to self-control and self-discipline. Knowing how to participate is part of the fabric contributing to a child's emotional security blanket. If you don't believe it, just think of a time when you went way over one of your deeply-held, behavioral limits or boundaries. I'm guessing you felt pretty much out of whack, discombobulated, maybe even thoughts of heading for the abyss. Well, it's that much worse for a child who's in the process of negotiating interactions and learning what it means to exercise self-control, determine boundaries, limit behavior, and to act appropriately.

Teachers need to help students become skilled in the 3 R's:
Reasonable – Respectful – Responsible.

And, above all,

Teachers need to be:
Fair – Firm – Consistent.

Look within.
Within is the fountain of good,
and it will ever bubble up,
if thou wilt ever dig.

~ Marcus Aurelius

Catch 'Em Being Good

Sometimes, children hear few positive statements about themselves from others and, yet, all students benefit from well-placed praise. You, their teacher - their second parent - can fill the void and make every effort to observe and voice your recognition of a student or class behaving appropriately. Students benefit from experiencing the positive perceptions of an adult in so many ways. The teacher also has the benefit of increased opportunities for positive interactions and the strengthening of relationships with students. It can take less than ten seconds to acknowledge the positive actions of a student; but, the investment to emphasize the positive can reap the kind of reward that reduces classroom management obstacles. It can even bring a long-past student back to your class just to say, "You were one of my favorite teachers." Now there's a big, complementary plus!

I'm convinced that every child has something that qualifies for the "Catch 'Em Being Good" citation. However, be sincere in your praise and its application. Kids have an uncanny way of spotting genuine versus contrived. Catch 'em being good but make sure it's purposeful and authentic.

Is This Important?

Students will place value and emphasis on, guess what----what you value and emphasize. For example, assigning journal writing and, then, hardly referring to it, running out of class time, and/or forgetting to ask students to share their journal writings, and it won't be long before students forget, do not allocate time, and even skip journal writing altogether. In other words, students are as interested or as uninterested as you are.

Make sure you are as keen about class projects and assignments as you want your students to be. In doing so, they won't have to ponder, "Is this important?" Your demonstrated value, emphasis, and enthusiasm will make it obvious that, "Yes, it is."

Correct Those Papers

Correcting student work demonstrates the importance of the assignment. It also shows a personal interest in the student and a commitment to his or her academic success. The major advantage for the teacher is that correcting student work provides a window into the student's thought process, strengths and weaknesses, and academic progress. There are many strategies for correcting student work. Take advantage of web-based suggestions, Best Practices, and the suggestions of veteran teachers to develop a variety of techniques for correcting student work. After all, if there is no teacher feedback, what's the use of doing the assignment?

The Challenger (Make Them Think)

T: "What else might the story characters have done to resolve this?"

S: "I'm not sure - what do you think?"

T: "It doesn't matter what I think; what do you think?"

This originated with my dad. I was a teenager and we were discussing something; I can't even remember what it was. When stuck for an answer, I asked what he thought. He answered, "Never mind what I think; what do you think?" That's the part I always remembered and it went with me, right into the classroom.

Don't settle for students abandoning their search for answers, prematurely, with, "I don't know?" Lead student to clarify, get specific, and dig for the answer. Become skilled in using Socratic questioning. Give them time to answer. Don't become their enabler -- you know, the answer provider. Make them think!

One's mind, once stretched
by a new idea, never regains
its original dimension.

~ Oliver Wendell Holmes, Sr.

Inspire Them

Students, regardless of age, are unconstrained in their capacity to be inspired. Through actions of volunteerism, charity, or emphasizing opportunities for random acts of kindness, students will rise to the occasion.

Inspire their thinking, as well. Offer them something to "chew on," ideas, current events, values, worldly issues, oh, so many ways to inspire. A word of caution, however; accept all ideas, reaction, and opinions without judgment and insist classmates do the same. Make no attempt to impose your perspectives.

Be ever-mindful that your job is to expose and not to impose. You have gone through the major search of who you are and what you think. You've selected your modus operandi. Students are at the beginning of their exploration. You are privy to their process, their journey, if you will, just by letting them investigate ideas and participate in activities they might not have had the opportunity to explore but for you.

AH, YES! The freedom to think, to express, to act -- And, might there be the next great of greats sitting in your class, right this minute; would it be concluded that you had something to do with it - would you have been the inspiration? In the moment, you never know where your influence might take your students because teaching's future impact is sealed in hindsight. It's a case of looking in the rear view mirror. You just never know where influence will end up.

Expectations

One of my earliest college professors, way back when, happened to say, "If you think you can or you think you can't—you're right!" At the time, I thought, "What a dumb saying." But, it's funny how growing older, older, and, still older relegates dumb sayings into pearls of wisdom.

Have high expectations for your students, for you, and for your chosen profession---teaching.

Expect the Best!

Things That Go Wrong . . . Often Make the Best Memories.

~ Gretchen Rubin

What's A Memory Worth?

What do we remember? Is it the Christmas presents we received when we were 5 years old, 10, or 13? How about the presents on our 8th or 12th birthday? We probably won't forget when we got our first pet, bicycle, or car; but, the rest, all those things that we couldn't live without, then, we most likely couldn't even remember what they were, today.

So what do we remember? What are the memory makers? They are the interactions we experience with those that mean the most to us; a family monopoly game, a snowball fight, some hilarious situation, or a conversation-- just the two of us, all become part of the fondest-memories inventory. We'd probably not remember what we got on a Christmas, long past, but we would remember practically all the details of a snowy day sliding down the highest, neighborhood hill on a saucer-sled with friends and laughing our heads off as we lost our grip, fell off, and went tumbling down the hill.

A former student recounts, "I remember when we had to catch the 5 white mice in Mr. J's 7th grade science class. I'll never forget the kid that set them loose and how the whole class went from trying to catch them to screaming and jumping on desks—just like in the movies. Mr. J really kept his cool and he was the one that finally got them back in their cage. The whole thing was so funny!" Now there's a memory for you. In a chance meeting with a former classmate, guess the topic of conversation? Right, the escaped white mice episode.

Memories create our sense of belonging. It's a form of bonding with the experiences of our world, the people we meet along the way, and those who influence us. Memories become our roots and add depth to who we are and where we've been. Thus, memories are a special and unique footprint in our lives. In reminiscing we recall memories that impacted our lives; perhaps they became our agent of change in some way or simply the cause of positive feelings.

Students are in school 180 days, approximately 7.5 hours a day, and for 13 years, maybe more—talk about opportunities for making memories.

The real art of conversation is not
only to say the right thing at the right place,
but, far more difficult still, to leave unsaid
the wrong thing at the tempting moment.

~ Lady Dorothy Nevill

Say What?!

Conversations with parents

I: DO
- A. Start with a genuine positive.
- B. Sincerely show respect and be friendly.
- C. Remember-you are talking about their flesh and blood; they might say it but you're not at liberty to do the same.
- D. Temper your words.
- E. Speak in understandable terms.
- F. Admit when you don't know something and offer to find out.
- G. Offer any and all help requested.

II: DO NOT
- A. Have a laundry list of complaints.
- B. Use derogatory, unsympathetic, or pointed words.
- C. Use teacher-speak or educational jargon.
- D. Demonstrate aloofness, arrogance, or superiority.
- E. Act like you know when you really don't.
- F. Be remiss in helping under the guise of, "It's not my job."

You can say just about anything if you know how to say it . . .

End of lesson!

IV: You're On— Break-A-Leg

Good Teaching is One-fourth Preparation and Three-fourths Theater

~ Gail Godwin

Your World Is a Stage

Enthusiastic

Creative

Adept in the Art

Exciting

Imaginative

Expert with the Script

Energetic

Animated

Embrace---Engage---Emote

Enjoy!

As you make your entrance, you'd be hard-pressed to find a bigger, better stage than the front of your classroom.

The Secret to Surprise
. . . is Humor.

~ Aristotle

"Just a Wild and Crazy Guy!"
Steve Martin

Incorporate the occasional surprise-- an impromptu activity, perhaps an unexpected guest, or something out-of-the-blue. Do something weird or bizarre once in a while-- tell a joke. Give them something to talk about, a "That was nuts!" kind of moment.

You'll be flabbergasted with the intensity of student observation in taking note of you, their teacher. They may even imitate you. You will be amazed when you hear a student repeat something you said or did that you would consider totally insignificant never suspecting it could have had an impact. Students will talk about class experiences and their impressions of you in and out of school.

A cardinal sin is to conduct a boring class and, even worse, to be boring. You know-- the kind of class where you'd rather be doing anything else, even the thing you least like to do would be better than sitting in that desk. Remember some of your college classes?

So, you don't tap dance and you can't sing, but you can still be entertaining from time-to-time.

Think what a better world it would be
if we all, the whole world, had cookies and
milk about 3 o'clock every afternoon and
then lay down on our blankets for a nap.

~ Barbara Jordan

All Grown Up—YIKES!!!

Maybe a daily dose of cookies, milk, and naps for adults might be a stretch, but keeping the child within - our inner child - is productive and beneficial on so many levels. First, we are working with children and to remember what it feels like to go through the process of childhood has to be a benefit to our students. Second, it keeps our creativity, imagination, and marvel alive. Finally, it's just more fun.

To quote Rebecca Pepper Sinker, "The reluctance to put away childish things may be a requirement of genius." Sounds about right.

Old teachers never die; they just never grow up.

You're On --- Break-A-Leg

So You Want to Be a Teacher   80

Justice-Oriented

The book, **A Road Less Traveled**, opens with, "Life is difficult." And, we all remember the early admonishments of, "Life isn't fair." But children are justice oriented. They are into fairness. Even if unable to verbalize their need for fairness, that's what they seek. When students complain, "They should do something." **They**, means the adults. Students look to the adults to deliver justice. As teachers, we are the mediators of justice. In doing so, we not only fill a need, we are also teaching lessons in negotiating, compromising, debating, evaluating, the art of winning, and the acceptance of losing.

As adults, we acknowledge the inequities of life, the shades of grey, which children have yet to recognize. Maintaining a justice oriented perspective works for us because it is fact based. It works for students because they feel they have a voice and a wiser, more experienced person will listen with an objective ear. We don't need to become a King Solomon, but we can strive to conduct a classroom that is fair and just for every student.

In learning you will teach,
and in teaching you will learn.

~ Phil Collins

Teacher and Student

Teaching credentials are only as good as Continuing Education. We teach - we learn; we teach - we learn; we teach - we learn. It's an unending circle.

Teachers need to be life-long learners, willing learners, excited about learning, and open to new ideas. And, sometimes, it's the students that become the professors.

What Is This Thing Called "Research?"

At some level, research is biased just by the mere fact that what is being investigated originated from an idea of the researcher. The level of influence within the exploration is impacted by how much a researcher embraces his or her ideas and the level of objectiveness and openness surrounding an investigation. This is not to say that we should dismiss research and its findings. However, rebuttals should be as important to consider as the research results.

Evaluate other theories that serve to rebut. Make your decision to adopt or reject from an objective examination of the various conclusions. Don't take research hook, line, and sinker simply because someone considered to be an expert in the field conducted the study. There are examples of research outcomes that eventually proved ineffective, even a disadvantage.

If you jump on a research bandwagon without serious evaluation, you might be heading in the wrong direction.

Surround yourself
with only people who are
going to lift you higher.

~ Oprah Winfrey

Who Are You Hanging With?

You probably heard the old adage: "Tell me who your friends are and I'll tell you who you are." There's some truth in that but maybe a more accurate analogy would be: "Tell me who you hang with and eventually you'll be influenced." If you are in the company of complainers, negative commentators, and the unenthusiastic crowd, sooner or later you will get with the program and join the discouraged and disillusioned.

The work of a teacher is not easy but, regardless, it requires an altruistic, generous, and charitable spirit; one that is positive and recognizes that there will be good and not so good days and that maybe every student cannot be reached but trying doesn't stop.

It's important for the sake of one's mental health and positive outlook to associate and develop relationships with colleagues that are unequivocally dedicated to the teaching profession and genuine in their commitment to working with children.

A 'No' uttered from the deepest conviction is better than a 'Yes' merely uttered to please, or worse, to avoid trouble.

~ Mahatma Gandhi

The Advocate

How much conviction? How much courage? Will you stand up for the students, for the profession, for education? Will you defend, comply, or concede? Will you refuse to live your career lukewarm? How are you, Advocate?

Sympathy Versus Empathy

Is there a difference between sympathy and empathy, and does it matter? Even though closely aligned, does each have its separate influence? Does clarifying the difference result in a more effective approach towards the student experiencing a sorrowful event? Here's the premise for you to decide whether or not the distinction has merit.

Sympathy has to do with feelings—yours. It has to do with expressions of sorrow, "I'm so sorry," is the usual first response, almost an apology for what the impacted person is experiencing. Sympathy is often relegated to experiences that cannot be restored, retrieved, or renewed and is an offering of comfort, the demise of a pet turtle for example. Although suggestions and advice can evolve, sympathy primarily remains in the "so sorry" arena. Its direction is not as much towards the recipient of sympathy as it is towards your feelings in recalling a similar experience and recounting how you dealt with the situation. The English novelist, George Eliot, said it this way: "Sympathetic people often don't communicate well, they back reflect images which hide their own depths." And, the British poet and painter, William Blake, offers: "Can I see another woe, and not be in sorrow too? Can I see another's grief, and not seek for kind relief?"

Sympathy is the reaction to another person's situation.

Empathy, on the other hand, is the ability to feel what the recipient of your concern is feeling. It is about the distressed person and has little to do with how you are feeling about the situation. It is from the perspective of the saddened rather than from your perspective. It is based in understanding and in giving voice to the impacted person. We've all heard, "Walking in his or her shoes." The Swedish writer, John Lindqvist, offers the insight: "Be me a little." And, from the Pakistani writer, Moshin Hamid, "Empathy is about finding echoes of another person in yourself."

Empathy moves away from sympathy and the "I'm sorry" statements and towards an offering of solutions. For example, not making the cut for the basketball team can become a student's angst-producing event. However, once the student is given a voice and his or her depth of disappointment and perspective is understood and acknowledged, the opportunity for investigating solutions and moving forward becomes a possibility.

Empathy is understanding the emotions and feelings of another person.

Sympathy and empathy are charitable and powerful human emotions. Knowing the difference along with how much and when to apply them is central to using sympathy and empathy effectively.

So what do you think?

Definitely—Maybe—Never Again!

There will be lessons taught and experiences experienced; some will rise to the level of, "Fantastic - where did that come from?" Others, with a little tweaking, will be really excellent; and some, not so much no matter what you do. Keeping a Definitely-Maybe-Never Again journal helps evaluate and prepare for the current and following school years.

A journal can also become a history of your day-to-day teaching. You might wonder why that could be helpful. Well, almost all of the films featuring the experiences of teachers are based on true stories.

You just never know where this profession called teaching will take you!

Rejuvenate

Some days, you'll find yourself dragging home and, once there, just unable to get off the couch. There will be certain times of the year when you feel no less than totally spent. You'll almost beg the universe to restore "the start-of-school, enthusiastic, you." You'll ask, "Where is ME? Where did I go? Who am I?"

Here's a clue; it's time to pump it up. Your enthusiasm, pump it up. Your energy, pump it up. Your strength, pump it up. "How?" you ask. Develop leisure-time activities, that's how. Now's the time to find your renewables and hang on to your kind of fun and relaxation. Teaching is intense and having outlets is vital to your well-being. Find your red carpet, pampering spa, love-to-do, king or queen for the day events and dive in---REJUVENATE!

"All work and no play...." — we all know where that ends up.

What's This Called?

- Is teaching a profession or not?

- Is teaching a calling or not?

- Are teachers born or cultivated?

- They call me, Teacher. What does that mean?

Each of you will have to find the answers within yourself.

A Million or Bust

Not to burst your bubble, but teaching won't put you in line to become a millionaire. However, if you jump out of bed in the morning and can't wait to start your day, then you found your million dollars, your destiny, that is. Find your passion wherever it takes you; that's where a fulfilled life resides and if it's teaching, the rest will follow including the finances.

Besides, as a teacher, there are built-in ways to increase financial wherewithall, for example, furthering education, taking on related responsibilities, or turning a hobby into something marketable. There are other benefits. A career in teaching is family-friendly, offers time to pursue interests, has intermittent downtime, and, in your classroom, you're chairman of the board.

And, after you've experienced those magical moments or an extraordinary, fantastic day, when everything fell into place, you will walk out of school at day's end and feel like a million bucks!

Who's on First?

Early on in my teaching career, I had a principal that would welcome the students as they entered school. She would greet the children with a smile and often pat them on their head. She was especially cordial to those from a large family. She was genuinely pleased to welcome each child, each day, with an enthusiasm that was contagious. One day, I asked her how it was that she eagerly met and greeted the children every single day. It was time-consuming and, as principal, she had so many responsibilities. She replied, "Without them, there's no need for any of us." I've often thought of her words throughout my career and have concluded that her simple statement was beyond profound. Regardless of the educational credentials or positions attained by the adults, the educational hierarchy, or those that influence, there would be no reason for any of it if it weren't for who's on first-----the children.

I have no desire to suffer twice,
in reality . . . and then in retrospect.

~ Sophocles

Hindsight

Have you thought of the exact thing to say long after the conversation has concluded? How about the perfect action, but, again, after the situation is long past? Hindsight, right! We've all been there.

As a teacher, there comes a time when you will say the wrong thing or take the wrong action—it happens. DO NOT BEAT YOURSELF UP! Rehearse what you would say or do in a similar situation, next time. Use hindsight to help hone your skills. After all, we all make mistakes, no matter the profession and even though we want to become the best possible teacher that doesn't have to include seeking sainthood. Things happen; we're human!

Hope and Faith

Parents bring a child into this world and begin an experience of the unknown. Teachers continue the process of the unknown as they conduct their classes.

Accepting these unknowns, with a willingness to forge ahead, launches a journey of courage and within courage resides the hope and faith that we can raise children who are more secure, than not; more happy, than not; and more capable, than not.

The courage of parent and teacher also embraces hope and faith in:

   . . . the next generation.

   . . . the ability to produce the next citizen.

   . . . providing the next work force.

   . . . preserving the country.

We need to be ever-mindful that we are not only raising children, we are also raising future adults and, as each new generation takes its turn, it does so with the underpinnings of the courage, hope, and faith generated by the previous generation of parents and teachers.

Teach me to feel another's woe,
To hide the fault I see:
That mercy I to others show,
That mercy show to me.

~ Alexander Pope

And One More -- Mercy

The parent's hope -- the student's process -- the teacher's accepted, unspoken covenant with parent and student, reminds us that we are all in need of compassion and mercy in our respective roles.

Who knew that a soliloquy written by Shakespeare would follow me into my career as a teacher? Well, this one did:

> **"The quality of mercy is not strained;**
>
> **It droppeth as the gentle rain from heaven,**
>
> **Upon the place beneath.**
>
> **It is twice blessed;**
>
> **It blesseth him that gives and him that takes."**

~ William Shakespeare
(1564-1616)

Do No Harm.

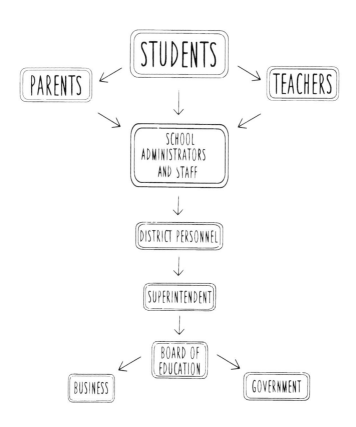

Made in the USA
Charleston, SC
09 March 2016